The Guiding Light

Other titles in the
Treasures of Inspiration series

HOPE IN DARKNESS
Poems of Sorrow and Comfort

YOUR HAND IN MINE
Poems of Love and Friendship

FROM THE HEART
Poems of Praise and Thanks

THE GUIDING LIGHT

Poems of Faith and Hope

Antioch Publishing Company
Yellow Springs, Ohio 45387
0-89954-777-X

CONTENTS

Marilyn Ashcroft, *The Guiding Light* 6

Laurence Ager, *The Cattle Byre* 7

John Bridge, *A Perfect Trust* 8

Dorothy Munt, *Where Is God?* 9

L. F. Rice, *Faith* 10

Hazel Bishop, *Count Your Blessings* 11

Marilyn Ashcroft, *Living in the Light* 12

Anne Hadley, *Teach Me* 13

Lyn Bevan, *The Old Cross and Chain* 14

Marilyn Ashcroft, *See the Stars* 15

Hazel Bishop, *Take Heart* 16

Marilyn Ashcroft, *The Peace of God* 18

Kevin Dean, *A Prayer* 19

Angela Upton Cheney, *Fields at Evening* 20

Joan Manning Wesson, *Prayer in May* 21

Peter Fenwick, *Joseph* 22

W. Emery, *The Hand of God* 23

Marilyn Ashcroft, *In His Presence* 24

Anne Hadley, *Think* 25

Marilyn Ashcroft, *The Dark Path* 26

Sister Imelda King, *Connemara Donkey* 27

B. F. Burgess, *Little Flowers* 28

J. Dalmain, *Have No Fear* 29

Shelagh Gemmel, *Because We Cannot See*   30

Marilyn Ashcroft, *Simple Trust*   31

Hazel Bishop, *God Answers*   32

Anne Hadley, *You Gave Me Hope*   33

Patricia Hadgifotis, *Renaissance*   34

E. M. Ashton, *Resurrection*   35

Sister Imelda King, *Palm Sunday*   36

Shelagh Gemmel, *Rebirth*   38

Anne McAndrew, *A Prayer*   39

Anne Hadley, *Revealed*   40

L. MacDonald, *A Moment in Time*   41

Edmund O'Gorman. *The Knight*   42

Thomas Foy, *My Angel Guardian*   44

L. MacDonald, *I Sought You*   45

Sylvia Moen, *I'm Lonely Again*   46

Glenda Mitchel Palmer, *The Prayer of a Parent*   47

Katherine Osborne, *Listen and Love*   48

Gaynor D. Williams, *Lifeline*   49

L. F. Rice, *A Soldier of the King*   50

Joanna Monks, *If You're Afraid*   51

Paul M. Pearson, *The Rain Is Falling*   52

Gaynor D. Williams, *Trust in His Loving Care* · 53

Myra Reeves, *Eliza's Window*   54

Frank Douglass Perry, *The Last Journey*   56

THE GUIDING LIGHT
Marilyn Ashcroft

Into the valley of shadow
You come as the guiding light.
You take our hand and lead us on,
Safe through the darkest night.

In all of our lives there are trials,
And times when we're in doubt,
We all need someone to turn to,
A friend who can help us out.

So let us ever remember,
Your presence is with us alway.
You promised Your help and comfort,
Your guidance each time we pray.

Through all our trials You take us,
Strengthening us every day.
Showing Your love and faithfulness,
Deepening our faith on the way.

THE CATTLE BYRE
Laurence Ager

The men who built the cattle byre
That sheltered Mary and God's son,
Could not have known their rustic skill
Would be renowned and glorious still
When centuries had run.

The manger framed by roughened hands,
Where Christ was laid in shadowed gloom,
A country carpenter had made,
A product of his daily trade,
And never guessed for whom.

So we, who in our daily work
Can fashion great or humble things,
May trust, though how we cannot say,
That what we labour at each day
May serve the King of Kings.

A PERFECT TRUST
John Bridge

O for the peace of perfect trust,
My loving Lord, in Thee;
Unswerving faith that never doubts
Thou choosest best for me.

Best, though my plans be all upset,
Though weary days be mine;
Cut off from much that others have,
Not my will, Lord, but Thine.

Best, though my earthly store be scant,
Best, though the way be rough,
Best, though my health and strength be gone,
In Thee I have enough.

And e'en though disappointments come,
They, too, are best for me –
To wean me from this changeful world
And lead me nearer Thee.

O for the peace of perfect trust
That looks away from all;
That sees Thy hand in everything
In great events and small.

That hears Thy voice, a father's voice,
Directing for the best;
O for the peace of perfect trust,
A heart with Thee at rest.

WHERE IS GOD?
Dorothy Munt

You ask me, 'Where is God?'
Come with me and I will show you.
Tread gently with care.
Can you clasp the rose fragrance from the air,
Or the breeze that rustles through the bough?
This is where His spirit walks with men.

FAITH
L.F. Rice

We will ring out the bells
Of faith, hope and love.
Lord, I believe.
According to your faith
It shall be done unto you.
Faith laughs at impossibilities,
Lays hold on real life,
Lets go what is useless,
Flees and follows and fights,
Removes mountains,
Opens doors, obtains promises.
Though small as a grain of mustard seed,
Yet, if placed in Almighty God,
Works wonders.
Looks to the Cross
And forward to the coming King.

COUNT YOUR BLESSINGS
Hazel Bishop

However hard the going is,
However bleak it seems,
Just keep on trusting Jesus,
He will fulfil your dreams.

And though the way seems dark and drear
And everything goes wrong,
Stay by the side of Jesus,
For that's where you belong.

So keep on trusting as you go
Along life's troubled way.
Just keep your eyes on Jesus,
He'll turn the night to day.

So praise Him for the good and bad
And count your blessings now.
For He will never leave you –
That's His eternal vow.

LIVING IN THE LIGHT
Marilyn Ashcroft

Living in the light means walking in God's sight.

So easy to say, but much harder to do,
For this life has so much to offer to you.
The world all around is an attractive place,
The decisions you make are so hard to face.

Living in the light means doing what is right.

Openness and honesty are the gifts you need,
So people know that they can trust your word
    and deed.
For acts of disrepute can't stand the light of day,
They find the darkest place to hide themselves
    away.

Living in the light means be prepared to fight.

The devil is so subtle with his snare,
Tread carefully and always be aware,
He is the skilful master of disguise,
Don't let his cunning take you by surprise.

Living in the light means trusting in His might.

His power can stop the devil in his tracks,
And give the faintest heart the strength it lacks.
His Spirit lives within you day by day,
To help you walk the straight and narrow way.
His love will hold you tightly if you fall,
And bring you home in triumph after all.

TEACH ME
Anne Hadley

Teach me the confidence of my own direction.
Concern for others as my only cue.
Keep me in the right direction
In my ever-searching quest for You.

THE OLD CROSS AND CHAIN
Lyn Bevan

Slowly I turned it in my hand,
The cross and chain that was made by hand.
As I held it and felt its warmth
I thought of the joy it must have brought
To someone in a bygone age,
But still the message rings out today,
For the cross and chain will always be
A symbol for prosperity.

If only life could just stand still
At some appropriate time,
When every day is fragrant and bright
And the sun seems to shine all the time.
But life cannot stand still, and to live it we must
Have our share of its heartaches and fears,
For we never could help another's sad heart
If we hadn't known tears through the years.

When a flower opens to the sun
We know that God's work has been done,
So it is, for you to see,
God's mighty hand is laid on thee,
And like the flower turned to the sun
Your spirit will lift.
God's work will be done.

SEE THE STARS
Marilyn Ashcroft

See the stars up in the sky,
The sun, the moon, the planets high,
Each one of them way out in space,
Our God has given it a place.

And so within God's master plan
There is a place for everyman.
A place that only he can fill
As he seeks to do the Father's will.

TAKE HEART
Hazel Bishop

Have you reached a point
   where you cannot cope?
Are you at the spot
   where there is no hope?
Can I tell you, my friend,
   that I've been there too?
And there is a 'Someone'
   who can pull you through.

Could you put your trust
   in Him above,
Who is ready and willing
   and able to love?
He will comfort and keep you
   for evermore –
Our dear Lord and Saviour
   has opened the door.

Will you walk right inside
   and let Him do His part
Of restoring and mending
   your poor broken heart.

He loves you, He wants you,
   He needs you right now;
Just call on His name
   and your head humbly bow.

He will stand right beside you
   this very day,
And help blow the troubles
   and miseries away.
So take heart, my dear friend,
   and do what I say –
Join hands with the Saviour
   and kneel down and pray.

I know what I'm saying,
   because I've been there too;
And today I am happy,
   contented – not blue.
Come join in the fellowship
   of God's family,
Rejoice with the Saviour
   and happy you'll be.

THE PEACE OF GOD
Marilyn Ashcroft

We often find we're searching for
The peace which God imparts.
Though we may not understand it
We can know it in our hearts.

It's more than just a quietness
It's more than peace of mind,
And there's nothing superficial
In this peace that we can find.

It permeates completely
Every fibre of our being.
It penetrates so deeply
And it's far beyond our seeing.

We do not need to understand,
We only need to know
The Father's promises are real
And that He loves us so.

God gave His reassurance
That He is always there,
And there's no need to worry,
Just turn our thoughts to prayer.

He promised to keep heart and mind
In close touch with the Lord,
As straight into our very lives
His peace would be outpoured.

A PRAYER
Kevin Dean

You touch the sun and give it glory,
You touch the stars and they are bright.
O, take my life's dull story
And fill it with Your light.
Every moment that you give me,
Success and failure too,
I offer back. Please make my life, Lord,
Something beautiful for you.

FIELDS AT EVENING
Angela Upton Cheney

This hour holds magic, when strange scents rise up
Out of the grass. . . . Beyond these pasturelands
The woods grow silent, shadowy, secretive:
Rooks have gone home, and in the quiet west
Some afterglow still lingers. . . . Up above
A single star pricks the fast-deepening blue
Like a cathedral lamp, and somewhere near
An owl calls to its mate. . . .
                       Pale ghostly flowers
Glimmer like pearls against the summer dusk,
And field-paths so familiar by day
Take on a meaning and a mystery
Undreamt in sunlight, with a subtle hint
Of some unnamed and undetermined realm
Waiting to be explored from where they melt
Into the gloaming. . . .
                    Now the tired earth
Yields gratefully to twilight's cool caress,
While in the half-light one becomes aware
Of hidden voices, other presences,
And things far back in time – a memory

Maybe, linked to one's inmost consciousness
With when the world was young, and in the still
Of evening, Adam walked and talked with God. . . .

So, when the long day ends for us, and when
Twilight gathers over the dewfall fields
And landmarks disappear, may it not be
That that is where we too meet up with Him?

Prayer In May
Joan Manning Wesson

Lord, heal me now with a vision of green things
   growing,
With the many shades of trees in a woodland
   way,
With delicate boughs that wave like waters
   flowing,
With the springing grass and the mountain corn
   and the may.

JOSEPH
Peter Fenwick

The son he loved was not his son,
The mother – set apart.
Alone God knows what awful doubts
Assailed his loving heart.

But, strong in faith, he heard the voice
That came from Heav'n's high throne,
And spent his life in toil and care
To keep them as his own.

And when death's angel laid his hand
Upon that tired, grey head,
God and His blessed mother knelt
In tears beside the bed.

God grant that we with equal faith
May walk the narrow way,
And come through tears and death's dark night
To bright, eternal day.

THE HAND OF GOD
W. Emery

The hand of God is always there,
Why not take it tonight?
Lift up your heart to Him in prayer
And tell Him of your plight.
Tell Him you feel you can't go on
And need Him by your side,
His love is everlasting
   and His arms are open wide.
Just pray to Him and ask His help,
And He will be your guide.

For He has trod that way before,
The way of bitter pain.
He knows your feeling of despair
And all your doubts and fears.
He will be with you to the end
And wipe away your tears.

IN HIS PRESENCE
Marilyn Ashcroft

There's a time every day
When we kneel down to pray,
And the cares of the day
Slip slowly away.

Then we give ourselves up
Into God's tender care,
And our hearts' deepest needs
Together we share.

In silent communion
We spend time with our Lord,
As into our hearts
His Spirit is poured.

Alone in His presence
We find sweet release.
In all of our problems
He gives us His peace.

There in the quiet
We always find grace,
And tenderest love
As we meet face to face.

THINK
Anne Hadley

Never destroy a bud,
Or you will lose
A flower.

Never waste a minute,
Or you will lose
The hour.

Always answer a question,
Which comes upon the
Mind.

Always give Him an
Answer,
Seek and ye shall find.

THE DARK PATH
Marilyn Ashcroft

When the path seems dark and long,
And you see no light at all,
You feel that God's deserted you
And He doesn't hear your call.

There seems to be no answer,
There seems to be no way.
You can't see a purpose
In your problems, come what may.

People may seem very kind,
And quite well-meaning too,
But do they really understand
Just what you're going through?

You find the quiet reassurance
Of those who really care,
Whose supporting hand of friendship
Is always ready there

Will help you through the darkness,
And point towards the light,
For Jesus holds the answer
But the time must not be right.

There's only one thing left to do,
And that's to trust the One
Whose plan and time are perfect,
And Who loves you as a son.

CONNEMARA DONKEY
Sister Imelda King

You looked forlorn,
Gazing down an empty road,
Standing there alone
As if looking into the past,
Seeing other roads
Beside pyramids and obelisks,
Palm branches and cheering crowds.
And yet I thought
Jesus would feel at home,
Finding you there
In my own countryside.

LITTLE FLOWERS
B.F. Burgess

Little flowers,
Arranged in such glorious splendour,
How come you dare
Hold high your heads so fair
As though the summer days
In which you bloom,
Entrancing all with your sweet perfume,
Stretched on for all eternity?
Why do you not weep
At the thought of your fall,
Which will come all too soon?
Why bloom at all?
For what, for whom?
Your splendour and your joy
  being so short-lived?

We bloom for Him, our creator,
And those, His creatures,
Who are able to reflect,
To translate the story
Of our transient but celestial glory.

That our glory be no more
Than a quick reflection
From eternity's mirror,
We have no care.
Nor do we concern ourselves
With whys and wherefores,
But merely live as He so wills,
To droop and die as He so desires,
Allowing fresh buds, fresh life,
To have their day,
Infinite creation
In which He never tires.

HAVE NO FEAR
J. Dalmain

Have no fear when you cannot sleep,
Or are unable to face life's way.
Pray – and beside you, God will keep
Every moment of night and day.

BECAUSE WE CANNOT SEE
Shelagh Gemmel

Crying for the world, Lord,
I'm crying for the world
I'm crying for the children
The children of the world
I'm crying in the poverty
The damp and cracking walls
I'm crying for the empty shelves
The broken cupboard doors
I'm crying in the stench, Lord,
Of rotting rubbish dumps
For drug-addicted mothers
And fathers on the dole
For sons in city riots
And daughters on parole
For stealing from the rich, Lord,
I'm crying for us all.

But most of all I cry, Lord,
Because we cannot see
That all we have to do
Is turn
To You
To be set free.

SIMPLE TRUST
Marilyn Ashcroft

Trust in the Lord with all of your heart,
And do not rely on your insight.
For God is the King, Lord of your life,
And wherever He leads you is right.

Trust in the Lord when the way seems so hard,
And nobody can understand,
For God is far greater than any one man,
He guides with His own gentle hand.

Trust Him completely for things yet to be,
For you know that the Lord will provide.
Yielding control into His tender hand,
Which way is for Him to decide.

But trust must be total, really complete,
And self must prepare to let go,
For God can't be Lord if you won't give in,
The depth of His love he can't show.

GOD ANSWERS
Hazel Bishop

God answers every prayer, you know,
However big or small;
And all He ever asks of us
Is that we make the call.

Just open up your heart to Him
And tell Him what you fear.
He's ready with the answer now,
He'll wipe away the tear.

So don't hold back, just call on Him,
And He will hear your plea.
God always keeps the promises
He made for you and me.

YOU GAVE ME HOPE
Anne Hadley

You gave me life,
Gave me hope,
Gave me love,
Through Your word
 I have them all.

Make me look,
Make me search,
Make me strive,
From that first
Faltering step
To Your side.

Make me search in my
Footsteps to You.
Keep me steadfast,
In each day
Anew.

RENAISSANCE
Patricia Hadgifotis

I was born in the summer of my twenty-fourth
   year,
Like a phoenix emerging from the flame
I arose from the ashes of my life;
Like summer bursting out of winter's chill
So love exploded out of my frozen heart.

A long, cold, hard winter it had been,
No warmth, no joy and no pity seen.
When suddenly out of the darkest watches of the
   night
An encounter that changed my lonely life,
With one that filled my heart with joy.
A going down and a rising up
To life renewed with hope and love.

I have known that chill of winter since,
But none so dark or so empty.
Short and bitter-sweet, pain touched with
   ecstasy.
And always consolation in a presence
   half-perceived;
Hiding there, yet only waiting to be sought out.

Now I stand in the spring of a new year,
Examining the tender buds of new life
   expanding
With the discovery of many new ways
And my eyes rest to the gentle kiss of light upon
   my face
And warm spring rain waters my thirsty soul.

RESURRECTION
E.M. Ashton

Damp, dark earth, cold as the grave,
Life lies buried, deeply contained.
But life cannot, will not be constrained.
As He emerged from His tomb,
Life bursts, blossoms, blooms
White, bright and pure.
Birth, death, rebirth, life evermore.

PALM SUNDAY
Sister Imelda King

They brought their gifts,
The halt, blind, retarded, dumb . . .
Shepherded
By parents, helpers, friends,
The celebrant a smile for all.

One lay oblivious,
Unresponsive,
Loving hands
The twitching, spindly legs
Held still,
Yet no sign . . .

The final hymn,
'Lord of the Dance';
Rose from her seat
A Down's Syndrome 'child',
Lumbered out,
Golden palm held high,
She bowed,
Swayed, lowered the palm,
Raised it,
Then suddenly with gay abandon

The ungainly feet
Began to dance,
Slowly keeping time
With flutes and guitars,
Gathering momentum,
The feet moved with grace.

We gazed in awe
At the rapturous face,
The eyes alight,
Ecstatic joy.

The music stopped . . .
She lumbered back.

No one stirred . . .

We had pitied her,
She with so little,
We with so much,
We were left pondering . . .

Did someone dance
With her there,
Adjust her steps to His,
And gently lead her . . . ?

REBIRTH
Shelagh Gemmel

You came
As I lay dying.

You came,
Lifting me gently away
As I watched myself lying there,
Dying there.

You came
Not in any recognisable form.
I knew it was You
I knew without doubt
It was my Lord
My loving Lord.
(I had not really known You before,
I had not even known to ask for help.)

You came.
Such love as I had never known
Enfolded me.
I had no fear.

A PRAYER
Anne McAndrew

As my words rise
With the smoke from the candle,
Open my heart, Lord,
To Your presence.
Burn away my sin.

As the wax melts
In the heat of the flame,
Soften my heart, Lord,
Through Your presence.
Mould me to Your will.

As the flame fades,
Leaving only the darkness,
Let me find peace, Lord,
In Your presence.
Change my fear to love.

REVEALED
Anne Hadley

Quickness of speech,
Soundness of vision,
These things tell me Jesus is risen.

Son of the Saviour,
Born of mankind,
World grieves without Him,
We're left behind.

Jesus is risen,
Son of mankind.
So, kindred spirits, don't
Dread the night.
Jesus is with you, you'll see the light.

Bible as comforter,
Servant and guide.
He'll always be there,
Saviour and friend.

A MOMENT IN TIME
L. MacDonald

Is there a moment in time
When God chooses the night to fall
And death to embrace us all?

Is there a moment of truth
When each one of us,
At our most heroic
And most noble,
Is called by Him?

Is there a moment of love
When we know ourselves
Most truly
For what we really are?

And in this moment
Of profound humility,
Contrite and in love,
We can finally acknowledge Him
And know Him as our own greater glory.

THE KNIGHT
Edmund O'Gorman

A knight of old in a castle dwelt,
All from the world apart,
With his brother knights and his Holy Rule
And his garden for his art.

And an old and feeble knight was he,
Who years crusading spent,
Who, since his life to battle gave,
Was little to learning bent.

A good man, sure, but knew no prayers,
His brain was like a sieve!
Yet glad he was when efforts made
Could a prayer to the Virgin give.

'Ave Maria' was all he'd say
From morning until night;
'Ave Maria' his watchword was
At work or in the fight.

Over and over and over again
These words came from his heart;
The other knights discarded him –
Their meaner counterpart.

He could not chant the choir with them,
He could not read a line;
Was slightly deaf and almost blind –
But 'ave-d' mighty fine.

Nor yet he ever said a word
In rash or useless vein;
He tended all the garden plots
Until he thence was ta'en.

For death did claim him peacefully,
His dying words were e'er,
'Ave Maria', as in life,
His one last loving prayer.

And when the spring came round again,
His grave the grass o'ergrown,
Surprised were the knights and brothers there,
For his sanctity was shown.

For from within his loving heart
A pure white lily bloomed
And saved his grave, by carelessness
And negligence foredoomed.

In letters of gold appearing on
That lily flowering there,
Was Mary's tribute to her child,
That knight's one earthly prayer: 'AVE MARIA'.

MY ANGEL GUARDIAN
Thomas Foy

Angel sent by God to guard me,
On life's pathway day by day,
Guide my footsteps every moment
Lest J stumble on the way.

Keep my eyes forever turned,
Upwards towards the face of God.
Leave me not till time is ended,
And all life's weary way is trod.

I SOUGHT YOU
L. MacDonald

I sought You in words
And found in You, Silence.

I sought You in darkness
And found in You, Light.

I sought You in reasons
And found in You, Truth.

I sought You in books
And found in You, Spirit.

I sought You in conflict
And found in You, Peace.

I sought You in stillness
And found in You, Life.

I sought You in solitude
And found in You, love.

I'm Lonely Again
Sylvia Moen

It isn't because I don't know You're there,
Or that You haven't heard my prayer,
It's just that I feel nobody cares,
And yet that's not true, so what shall I do?

When hours and days and weeks pass by,
And I'm still alone and sometimes cry,
Because the loneliness gets too much,
When there's no one there to love or touch.

What would You want me to remember?
Ah yes! That Your love is strong, yet tender,
That You're willing to come and ease the pain –
And get me back together again!

THE PRAYER OF A PARENT
Glenda Mitchel Palmer

Heavenly Father,
As Your little child,
Help me learn
To trust You to lead me.

But more,
Guide me as I lead my child:

That I may teach him not
'To stand on his own two feet',
But that I may help him learn
On Whom to lean.

LISTEN AND LOVE
Katherine Osborne

Whom shall I speak to, Lord,
When my heart is filled with pain
And a thousand sad anxieties
Torture my aching brain?
Oh Lord, let me speak to Thee
In words that seek only Thy love.
Let me lift my eyes and thoughts
To the peace of your realm above.

Whom shall I sing to, Lord,
When my heart is filled with joy,
And a thousand carefree, happy thoughts
Bring peace without alloy?
Oh Lord, let me sing to Thee
A song of love and praise,
And glory and hope and thanks
For these wonderful peace-filled days.

Whom shall I listen to, Lord,
When my heart is filled with doubt,
And a thousand clouds and shadows
Seem to shut the sunshine out?
Oh Lord, let me listen to Thee,
To Thy words that are gentle and sweet,
Till my anxious heart finds peace
At thy bloodstained, piercèd feet.

LIFELINE
Gaynor D. Williams

Hold my hand and guide me
Through the dark maze of despair.
Help me find tomorrow. . . .
Just let me know You're there.
For I must go alone, I know,
Through the whirlpools of the night,
Towards a grey tomorrow
Where only You will be my light.

A SOLDIER OF THE KING
L.F. Rice

I cannot tell whither goes the mighty sun,
That having made our day, forsakes our sky
To rise again, intent upon that glorious run,
What kindly power to move us from on high.
But this I know, that I enjoy the sunshine,
And long for love to fill this soul of mine.
That, as those warm rays gently urge and
    quicken,
I yet may know something of light divine.

I cannot journey up among celestial beams,
Or find rare pearls upon the ocean bed
Or venture out, beyond where sunset golden
    gleams,
To hail our brethren, yellow, black and red,
But this I know, that I can stay and gladden
Or cheer or comfort some lost anxious soul
And make some hearth a bright and cheerful
    evening
And feel that yet I have not missed the goal.

I could not plan a lofty Concorde aeroplane
Or spin a cobweb in the morning air
Or dig a Channel Tunnel for the Dover train
Or plant a forest cool and green and fair.
But this I know, that I can rise up early
And run and shout and laugh like anything,
And humbly look to see what I can do
As one who is a soldier of the King.

IF YOU'RE AFRAID
Joanna Monks

If you're afraid and life gets you down,
Put on a smile and take off that frown.
There's always hope that things will improve,
So get to your feet and make a move.
If you hope and look you'll find the light,
So don't give up – put up a fight.
There's one little word which means you can cope,
And don't forget it – that word is hope.

THE RAIN IS FALLING
Paul M. Pearson

The rain is falling,
The air is fresh and cold,
I am alone,
The windows are faceless.

No, I am wrong,
I am not alone,
Deep down I know differently,
God is with me.

He is within me,
He is around me,
I am supported by Him,
Held in the palm of His hand.

My soul is at peace in Him,
God is within me,
He is Heaven itself,
And I have found Heaven.

TRUST IN HIS LOVING CARE
Gaynor D. Williams

When life is full of shadows,
Doubt, and dark despair,
Reach out and touch the hand of God –
Trust in His loving care.

At times it's hard to understand
Why life deals its bitter blows
Of pain and grief and loneliness,
To the young, the frail and the old.

The pattern of our lives, the way of things,
Is hard to understand,
But the light of hope *will* shine again –
If only we'll take His hand.

ELIZA'S WINDOW
Myra Reeves

Lean by this window at nightfall.
Dusk makes mysterious those rusty sheds,
The stark precision of the chapel's shell.
Throw back the leaded panes and lean a little,
Where on your left the crooked dormers jut,
Angled awry on the patched roof
   of this old house.

And to the right is scrawled
A faintly pencilled television toasting-fork
Where ring-doves sit and coo all day
Two long arm-lengths away.
You will see beauty too –
The far reach of sky
Cloud-whipped or moon-illumined,
Backcloth for that ethereal shape, the tower,
Four-square, high-pinnacled,
Symbol of man's upthrust to Heaven.

And a late dove flies over,
Close to your hand as the hand of a lover,
But transient.

You might think of God
Hovering over that chiselled loveliness.
But not look to where
You barely sense uneven roofs,
Here-and-there glimmer of window light,
Ghosts of chimney-pots pointing,
    blurred homesteads,
Where unheard voices mutter and call and cry,
Woman and child and man love, live and die,
Unseen, but felt, but known,
Welded with you.

If God is anywhere.
He is there.

The Last Journey
Frank Douglass Perry

When death doth come, as come it must,
And I return again to dust,
I hope my friends will think of me
As sailing on a sunlit sea
To harbour in a far-off land,
Where friends will take me by the hand,
And lead me to a quiet place,
To meet my dear ones face to face,
Before I pass the narrow gate
Which all must pass to know their fate.
From beggar's hut or from a throne,
That step which each must take, alone,
And then, I hope, my friends will pray
That I shall hear my Maker say,
'Your vanity and greed and pride
Are pardoned here, because you tried.'

Designed and produced by
Genesis Productions Limited
30 Great Portland Street
London W1N 5AD

Compilation copyright © Genesis Productions Limited 1986
Copyright in the poems is retained by the
authors or their assignees, © 1986
All rights reserved

First published in the United States of America 1987 by
Antioch Publishing Company

Designed by Bernard Higton
Printed and bound in Hong Kong by
Everbest Printing Co., Ltd.

ISBN 0-89954-777-X

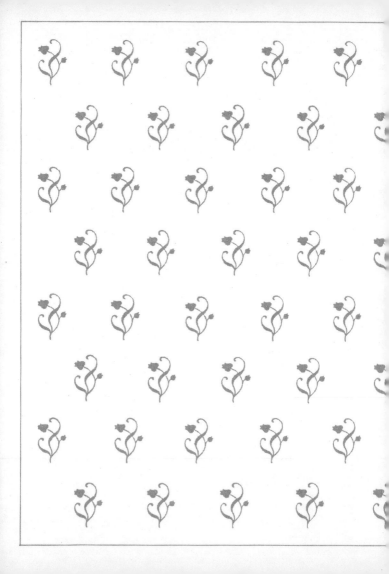